Saxophone

Matilda James

xist Publishing 

A Note to Parents & Teachers—

Welcome to Discover Musical Instruments from Xist Publishing! These books are designed to inspire discovery and delight in the youngest readers. Each short book features very simple sentences with visual cues to get kids reading for the first time.

You can help each child develop a lifetime love of reading right from the very start. Here are some ways to help a beginning reader get going:

- Read the book aloud as a first introduction
- Run your fingers below the words as you read each line
- Give the child the chance to finish the sentences or read repeating words while you read the rest.
- Encourage the child to read aloud every day!

First Edition

Published in the United States by Xist Publishing
www.xistpublishing.com
24200 Southwest Freeway #402-290 Rosenberg, TX 77471

eISBN: 978-1-5324-1697-2
Paperback ISBN: 978-1-5324-1698-9
Hardcover ISBN: 978-1-5324-1699-6

Table of Contents

This is a saxophone.

The saxophone is a wind instrument.

Wind instruments need moving air to make sound.

Saxophones have a reed and 23 keys.

Saxophones are made of metal.

I put the reed in my mouth to make sound.

I push the keys to change the sound.

Saxophones sound great in jazz bands.

Saxophones can be part of a band or an orchestra.

I can also play saxophone by myself.

I like to play the saxophone.

Photo Glossary

Key

Part of a musical instrument that changes the sound made

Orchestra

A group of musicians who play together

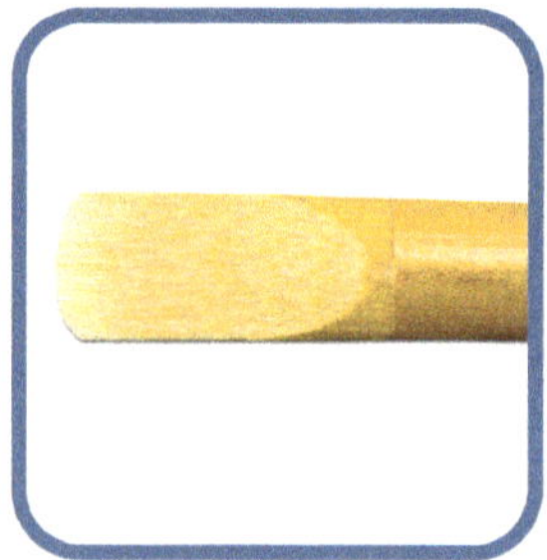

Reed

Thin strip of material that vibrates to make noise

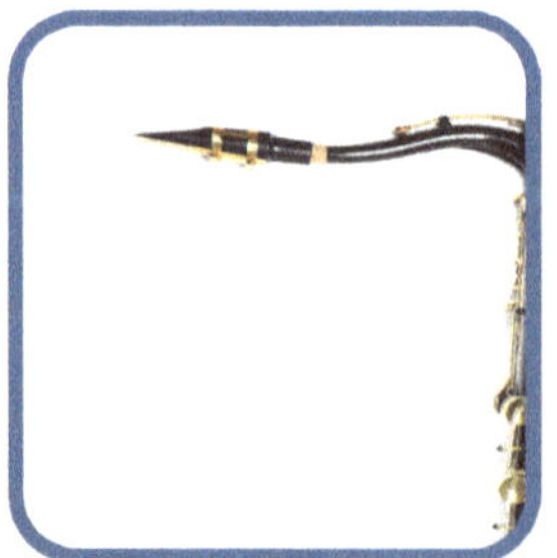

Wind Instrument

Type of instrument that needs wind to make noise

Things to do next!

Write a Sentence

Saxophones are ___________.

Drawing

Draw yourself playing a Saxophone.

Sharing

Tell your classmates about a musical instrument you have heard.

Index

www.ingramcontent.com/pod-product-compliance
Ingram Content Group UK Ltd.
Pitfield, Milton Keynes, MK11 3LW, UK
UKHW062300290726
14090UKWH00017B/798

9 781532 416989